Usborne
First Sticker Book
Trucks

Illustrated by Dan Crisp

Contents

There are lots of truck stickers at the back
of this book for you to stick on each page.

Words by Sam Taplin

Designed by Meg Dobbie and Matt Durber

In the country

Trucks drive slowly along the winding country roads, carrying animals and food. Tractors work in the fields.

In the town

Lots of trucks drive through the busy town. Fire engines zoom along the streets, and rubbish trucks collect the rubbish from the houses.

PIZZA PIZZA PARADISE

BUDGET WAREHOUSE

The Salon

SAM'S NEWS

At the factory

Big, heavy car transporters take away
all the cars that are made in this factory,
and forklift trucks move boxes.

On the motorway

Big trucks and small trucks roar along the noisy motorway. Rescue trucks come to help cars that have broken down.

Services

Services

The trucks on the
motorway carry all
kinds of different things.

At the building site

The building site is full of diggers,
dump trucks and concrete mixer trucks.
Skip trucks take away rubbish.

In the mountains

Some trucks have wheels with chains so they can drive through the snowy mountains. Gritter trucks and snow ploughs keep ice and snow off the roads.

At the port

Car transporters and petrol tankers arrive at the port.
Container trucks wait to drive onto ships.

STORAGE UNIT

0492

0492
CARGO HOLD

0492

0492
CARGO HOLD

Make your own picture

Use the stickers of trucks and buildings
to make your own picture on this page.

In the country

Milk truck

Horse truck

Hay bale truck

Cattle truck

Tractor and trailer

Jeep and horsebox

Quad bike

Vegetable truck

Grain truck

In the town

Fruit truck

Street sweeper truck

Car

Van

Fire engine

Rubbish truck

Removal truck

Market truck

Diesel tanker

Banana truck

At the factory

Forklift truck

3-car transporter

Flatbed truck

Curtainsider truck

9-car transporter

Forklift truck

Box truck

Articulated truck

Trailer truck

Forklift truck

On the motorway

Car

Flatbed truck

Removal truck

Container truck

Curtainsider truck

Milk truck

Rescue truck

Box truck

Petrol tanker

Container truck

Articulated truck

At the building site

Skip truck

Tipper truck

Dump truck

Crane truck

Flatbed truck carrying dump truck

Tipper van

Van

Digger

Concrete mixer truck

Skip truck

In the mountains

Snowmobile

Box truck with snow chains

Log loader truck

Jeep with snow tyres

Articulated truck with snow chains

Snowmobile

Gritter truck

Snow plough

Timber truck

Ski slope truck

Make your own picture